Marriage Is More Than You & Me

Reflections for Engaged Couples Entering Catholic Matrimony

Edited by Patrick E. Brennan

Marriage Is More Than You & Me
Reflections for Engaged Couples Entering Catholic Matrimony

Edited by Patrick E. Brennan
Artwork by Isz

Dedicated to all couples who have said "Yes"
to the sacrament of marriage.

Portions of this book were originally published in *Family Seasons* magazine and are used with permission. This book was developed by the Family Life Office of the Archdiocese of Hartford, Connecticut, in cooperation with *The Catholic Transcript*, the official newspaper of the Archdiocese. No part of this book may be reprinted without the express written permission of the publisher.

Printing 6 5 4 3 2 1
Year 1997 95 94 93 92
Library of Congress Catalog Card Number: 92-07828
ISBN: 0-915388-45-6
Printed in the United States of America.

CONTENTS

Acknowledgments

This book represents the culmination of years of reflection by people concerned that couples planning for marriage in the Catholic Church receive as much preparation and support as possible. Our hope is that couples will use this booklet and the varied marriage preparation programs available to take the necessary time to prepare for a lifelong commitment to a rewarding relationship.

Thanks go to the dozens of writers who have contributed to *Family Seasons* magazine over the past seven years, from which the content of this publication was largely derived; to the helpful staff at *The Catholic Transcript*, newspaper of the Archdiocese of Hartford, Connecticut; and to those who reviewed the manuscript of this book during the revision process. A note of appreciation also to the staff of the Family Life Office: Bunny O'Brien, Marie Smith, and Sister Mauryeen O'Brien, O.P. Special thanks to Don and Chris Paglia, parents extraordinaire and executive editors of *Family Seasons*, for their guidance, and to managing editor Louise Pyers, who spent countless hours coordinating the selection and revisions of articles for this book. A final note of thanks to my wife, Diane, who was of immense support during the editing and design.

Patrick E. Brennan

Introduction

Whenever we have thumbed through any of the popular bridal magazines, read the articles, and noted the various ads, photos, and other information they offer, we have been left feeling quite unsettled.

The principal goal of these magazines is to be a resource guide for couples who wish to have the "perfect wedding." This isn't a negative notion in itself, other than the fact that "perfect" is not reachable, nor even necessarily desirable. The problem is the inordinate amount of emphasis placed upon the *wedding* plans and the apparent lack of emphasis placed upon the subsequent *marriage*.

These magazines are designed to make money. They sell things. They sell gowns, rings, dinnerware, furniture, luggage, travel package honeymoon trips, and a life committed to materialism, sex appeal, and "take-your-breath-away beauty." Our difficulty with all this is context.

There is, of course, nothing wrong with a well-planned wedding day; nor, for that matter, with a reception and wedding celebration of large proportions—that is, if they are placed into the proper context. This means that the wedding celebration needs to point to the reality of what is truly happening with this union. It is actually a party to celebrate that "God loves his people." The husband and wife will express this divine love concretely—through words and deeds—as they live out their conjugal love.

Their bond of love becomes the image and symbol of the covenant that unites God and his people. This is wonderful. It is wonder-filled. It demands to be celebrated. And the need and desire to have a great wedding and wedding celebration is fitting.

Marriage is a social matter. It has always been an occasion of rejoicing that brings together families and friends. And it is also a sacrament. It is an ongoing process of sacrifice, compromise, raising a family, prayer, and dealing with the enjoyable and the annoying things of a life together. In marriage preparation we, like so many of you, operate on the belief that the popular adage, "Marriage is a lifetime," is not only true, but is universally held to be true. The bridal magazines we've viewed seem to ignore this idea.

Perhaps it makes sense to look at the motives of any wedding plans and ask basic questions, such as, "Why are we doing whatever we are doing?" "What is the purpose of our large, small, costly, intimate, formal, informal, etc., reception?" "Whom are we inviting? And why?"

In addition to making thoughtful and wise choices concerning the *wedding* plans, we encourage all couples to focus their major energies on the *marriage* plans. The wedding can often exhaust any couple. It is a lot of work. And the only reason it is worthwhile work is that it prepares us for the ongoing work of marriage that needs to continue long after the bills for the reception and gown are paid, and long after the honeymoon photos are placed into an album.

No, the bridal magazines don't say all this. They are exciting and fun to look at. But they don't give a clue to the excitement and fun in store for those blessed and courageous enough to invest in this lifelong journey of work and effort — this thing called marriage. We hope and pray that the selection of articles presented here from various authors will offer some balanced reading during the engagement and help with both the wedding plans *and* the marriage plans.

Donald and Christine Paglia
Co-directors

Family Life Office
Archdiocese of Hartford

Laying the Foundation

ONE

Marriage is more than you and me

Patrick and Diane Brennan

Did you know there is an "official" way to fold towels? That's right, and God forbid you get it wrong! Who knows, in the middle of the night they might mysteriously straighten out and fall off the shelf and get hurt!

Believe it or not, this was one of the many early disagreements in our marriage. We didn't realize it at the time, but our families of origin had followed us right into our first apartment—in the form of expectations of behavior we picked up when younger.

My mother (Patrick's) was usually so happy that someone would help her fold towels after they were laundered that she didn't care which way they were folded —just as long as they weren't rolled up in a ball and stuffed in the closet. Diane's mother, on the other hand, was very particular about how the towels were folded. By doing it a certain way, more of them could be compacted into a tight space on a closet shelf, thus leaving room for other things. This lesson was not lost on Diane.

So, what happens — our first big load of towels comes up from the washer and I (Patrick) promptly fold them while watching TV and put them back in the closet. I then sit back, relishing the nice kiss and hug I will receive when Diane sees how much I help out around the house.

Much to my amazement, I am called to the closet and receive a lecture and folding lesson from my wife. She then proceeds to pull all my folded towels off the shelf and spends the next twenty minutes getting them "just so." I sit elsewhere, wondering, "What did I do wrong?"

Seriously, newly married couples should expect numerous incidents like this as a direct consequence of merging two different life histories into one. Adjustments are to be expected in marriage; the only uncertainty is to what degree they will cause stress in the relationship. The situation isn't entirely negative either — partners notice each other adjusting and the blending has the potential to enhance their shared life.

This process, while quite evident among the newly married, continues throughout the marriage. When parents become grandparents, for instance, their mind switches back to their grandparents' behavior, adds in new life experiences and observations of other grandparents, and then formulates what kind of grandparent they want to be. Their partners go through the same process. They must then come to an understanding of how, or if, they want to present a united front to their new grandchild.

Adjustments occur in every part of a couple's relationship as their expectations of "how things should be in our marriage" meet head on with reality. Some of these expectations might be, "We'll never fight," "We'll have lots of sex whenever we want," or "We'll have children on our own time schedule."

When we look back to when we wanted our first child, our expectations were a little overdone. We decided we had to get pregnant in August, because we wanted a May baby so that Diane wouldn't be uncomfortable during the hot summer months. We also decided that our second year of marriage would be the right time. That was the expectation we shared.

The reality was quite different. After one year of marriage we moved to a different city five hundred miles away. Money was tight, Diane had health problems, and although we still got pregnant in August as we had wanted, it ended in a miscarriage a short time later. The emotional and physical scars took a long time to heal, and after several unsuccessful attempts a pregnancy was again achieved. By this time we didn't care what time of the year it was or what Diane would have to endure — we just wanted a baby. As it turned out, Diane did carry through the hot summer and Bridget was born in the September of our fourth year of marriage. So much for our expectations; reality demanded a lot of adjustments.

This was an example of expectations that ignore a basic fact: we are not as much in control of our own lives as we have been led to believe.

Our unrealistic expectation resulted in disappointment and frustration. But the opposite can also be true.

When expectations are realistic and then are exceeded, we can experience joy and happiness. For instance, we both thought that owning a home was a distant goal. I (Patrick) thought it was impossible, considering our income and the price of houses. We shared a pessimistic attitude about buying a home because of my expectations. Imagine our surprise when a change in circumstances and actually sitting down with a good real estate agent led to our purchase of a home when we had been married only three years! Even now we still can't believe it happened.

Both of these examples reflect on the fact that we had the same or very similar expectations in certain areas of our relationship. Sometimes couples have vastly different expectations, however, and dealing with them can lead to marital conflicts.

When a couple has different expectations, they can either each stick to their guns in the hope that the other will change, or they can decide to compromise. When they compromise, they either reshape their individual expectations or help each other achieve their individual goals.

Examples of areas where couples might clash involve expectations on the frequency of sex, the amount of money each partner can spend without consulting the other, and how household duties will be shared. Where do such expectations come from? Each of us enters marriage with individual influences and family histories. We have our own image of what we want our marriage to be like. We each are used to doing things the way our family did them.

The expectations we hold can be seen as a kind of legacy left to us by the generations that preceded us — embedded in our ethnic, religious, or socio-economic backgrounds. I (Patrick) need only think back to our wedding reception plans to see how individual legacies first came to light. My mixed but mostly third-generation Irish family was rather "laid back" and content to have a simple picnic reception under a tent in the back yard. Diane's mostly second generation full-blooded Polish heritage called for nothing less than a polka band and a formal indoor reception with what I thought were peculiar, but fun, ethnic and religious customs.

Our family backgrounds were exemplified in individual family portraits taken during the reception. Diane's family followed the photographer's directions and lined up nicely, all smiling and looking at the camera. My family portrait shows a true "happy party crowd" looking all over the room and telling jokes to each other while the hapless photographer tried to get their attention. Five years later, both families are still talking about our wedding. It was something of a family culture shock, something akin to what the Chinese thought of Marco Polo when he arrived in their country with his round eyes, European clothing, and strange manner of speaking.

Marital expectations are formed mostly by one's parents. We bring to our own marriages what we saw modeled in our homes. This is, in fact, so common that it has been said that in every marriage there are at least six persons: the bride, the groom, and their parents. Perhaps we should urge a rewriting of the marriage vows: "I, Diane, take you, Patrick, and also your mother, your father, and all of your family heritage. . . ."

Our families' influences on our expectations cannot be overlooked, even if we view ourselves as being very different from our parents or think that we have rejected their expectations. Research shows that family patterns are often repeated and family expectations upheld.

There are many conscious and unconscious ways in which couples repeat the patterns and preferences of their parents. We constantly observed what our parents did and heard what they said. In times of stress, when there's no time to think, we often revert back to *acting as our parents did*, rather than *acting as we would rationally like to act*.

When dealing with the expectations that have been passed down to us, married couples should stay away from blaming our parents. They did the best they could do for us. It is not as important to understand *what happened* in our childhood as it is to understand *how it has affected our behavior and expectations*. Keep in mind that the past is over. We need to learn from it, accept it, and move on with our own lives. The only reason to look back at the past is to understand it so that we can better understand ourselves and our spouses.

Today, expectations carried into marriage may not be as easy to identify as they were in the past. Some, such as the "proper" role of a husband or wife, are not as clearly defined for us. Each couple must examine their relationship to determine what they expect from it. An awareness and understanding of our expectations, however, helps us to deal with them. We can "use them or lose them," or we can change them to make them our own. But the cycle won't break unless we see them for what they really are.

Now, let's get back to folding towels.

DISCUSSION QUESTIONS:

1. Imagine you are carrying into your marriage a suitcase filled with "stuff" from your family of origin. What is one of the treasures? What is one of the burdens?

2. What are some of the expectations you bring to this marriage concerning meals (your picture of what a regular family meal should be like): the people involved in the preparation, what time it takes place, where it takes place, who sits at the table? Which expectation would be the most difficult to let go of? Why? Which would be the easiest? Why?

3. For the interfaith couple: What assumptions do you bring into your relationship regarding your own faith, your future spouse's faith? What special faith traditions do you bring with you from your own family of origin? What faith traditions do you want to carry on as a couple, and with your children?

TWO

This is a job for
the newly married

Donald Paglia

The wedding was only three weeks away. Mark and Susan had finished practically everything on their long list of items to complete for their wedding day. Mark had even convinced his best man to wear the tuxedo that Susan had wanted for the men. Everything and everyone seemed in fine shape. And then it happened.

What seemed like such a small detail — the seating arrangements for the reception — turned into a nightmare! Susan's mother went from being "pushy" to downright "hostile" over who was to sit where and with whom. Mother and daughter went at it with a passion, resulting in several family members taking sides and tempers flaring everywhere.

Susan found herself at Mark's apartment weeping and sobbing over the entire episode. How could her wedding day be so taken over by her mother? She felt miserable. Susan felt like a little girl who was not allowed to make her own decisions, not like a young adult woman about to be married.

Each of us brings to marriage so-called "unfinished business" and expectations that come from our own family background. After all, our family of origin is the primary model on which we will base our own newly established family — for better or for worse.

When we are newly married, we don't often think of ourselves as a family yet, but we really are. And we actually have specific tasks during this stage in our family's lifespan. This is the time for us to become a separate, but connected, unit of our extended family systems, and many of the adjustments in the first year of marriage center around each of us successfully leaving his or her own family and joining to become a married couple. This process doesn't happen overnight, but is a gradual one that requires time to occur.

For Susan this was not the first time that she had feelings of being controlled by her mother. What was different was that she thought (or rather hoped) that by getting married her relationship with her mother would change.

After several hours of talking with each other and with Mark's older married sister and brother-in-law, Susan and Mark began to see how their marriage must be the start of a new relationship with their own families of origin, and that this would be only the beginning of the changes that would need to occur. They also realized that both Mark and Susan would have to work on these new and changing relationships with their families that their wedding was formalizing but hardly completing.

What are some of the tools needed to accomplish this work of the newly married couple? Well, to begin, we need to develop a solid communication pattern with each other and with our respective families that will enable us to handle the conflicts and differences that arise. Also, we need to know that if we ignore this task there is a great risk of bringing into the next stage of our family life the same unfinished business and unspoken agendas, expectations and hopes, plans and problems with which our parents struggled.

It is vital that the primary task of this stage of family life be successfully completed: to become a separate but connected unit of our own respective family of origin. There is so much to be gained for the newly married couple in doing this work of becoming "separate but connected" with our family of origin.

For instance, we all come into marriage with several generations of traditions, myths, patterns, and issues that need to be reckoned with early in order for us to establish our own family. Things such as meal times, the way holidays are celebrated, what is or isn't appropriate in how we express affection toward each other in public — these are just a few of the things that we bring with us into marriage. In the area of decision-making, for example, the husband might enter into the marriage with a long-standing tradition that the man must make all of the important decisions.

He may have experienced his father—perhaps a grandfather, uncles, and brothers as well—as the decision-makers in his family. The wife may have entered into marriage with a family history of husbands and wives deciding issues together. This difference will directly influence their relationship.

The difficulty is that often these kinds of patterns and family traditions won't show up until well after the wedding. This is because most of us don't immediately face the potential problems that a lifelong commitment entails. For instance, his family may have yelled and shouted about things, while her family may have remained silent over issues. One may have come from a family that valued religious practice, while the other may have come from a family that attended church occasionally or seldom.

Eventually, things that are initially dismissed or overlooked prior to the wedding or in the honeymoon stage start to wear and become sources of frustration. All the wishful thinking, such as, "She'll stop visiting her mother so much" or "He'll stop working so much and spend more time with me," doesn't resolve anything. Soon the patterns that are so deeply rooted, but not previously discussed or acknowledged, start to become quite visible.

Trying to live out marriage with someone with different ways of doing things can bring on great stress because marriage necessitates trying to relate closely on a daily basis. This can cause us to create "triangles" as a way of handling the stress. Triangles occur in all families and tend to show up when the emotional atmosphere is intense. Whenever there is difficulty working out the balance in the one-to-one relationship, a married couple can "bring in" another person to offset the emotional intensity generated by the imbalance. We might do this by drawing someone else into a disagreement so that the issue gets less personal or the topic gets changed. Both of these approaches move a couple away from an emotionally charged issue.

Most of us get into these triangles, since there are lots of opportunities for them to occur. As our newly established family moves into the task of becoming a separate but connected unit of our own extended family systems, triangles can spring up all over the place. The patterns of our own family of origin can be a source of predicting some of these triangles: How did our own parents use triangles? How were we part of them? What were they used for? When did they surface?

Something normally and frequently experienced by many newly married couples is that one of the partners stays too close to a parent or parents, leaving the other partner out. Another triangle occurs at the birth of the first child. Here the shift is from marital dyad (husband and wife) to triad (wife, husband, and child). With the addition of each child, there is a need to do some restructuring and balancing of roles, responsibilities, and time. This movement into every new stage of family life can cause additional stress and difficulties, especially if stress related to the previous stage is still apparent.

The primary reason that triangles are difficult to avoid is that intimacy between a couple, however much it is pursued, is difficult to sustain. Triangles may be formed early in the marriage as the couple first tries to break away from their family of origin and build closeness with each other. As their intimacy builds, it can actually frighten them, and so they unconsciously calm down the intensity by creating the most common triangle in a marriage, which involves an in-law and two spouses.

So often we think it only the couple's task to separate from the family of origin. We must become our own persons, form close peer relationships, and pursue career-life plans. But this is only one half of the equation. Our parents must also let go of us. They need to recognize that we, as their adult married children, will now need to shift some of our loyalty from our family of origin to our new marital system. Parents who will not let their children do this can literally destroy a young couple's marriage.

All engaged couples need to see that their parents are going through a "disengagement" period. This tension is often seen in the turmoil that can be created over the newly married couple's problem about where to eat a holiday dinner — his parents? her parents? both? neither?

Some writers describe our major task in life as that of "leaving home." For the newly married couple this task is expanded and continued. The couple must work on the developing of their marital system and the realigning of their relationships as a team or unit.

Marriage preparation classes and programs and engaged couples encounters are all very helpful, but it is important to remember that the learning and the work need to continue after the wedding. Every couple ought to consider counseling if they come up against issues that they cannot handle on their own.

There is no question that in the committed relationship of marriage, we have the real opportunity to grow and mature. In this growing and maturing we can find happiness and the face of God. Marriage is not something that we do once and for all. Rather, it is a process, a "job" in the true sense of the word, something that must be worked at actively every day. In order for a marriage to be successful, there must be an openness to seeing marriage and family life as a lifelong process of growing and becoming. This is the primary job of the newly married couple.

DISCUSSION QUESTIONS:

1. What is the most difficult aspect of "leaving home" for you? The easiest?

2. Is there any unfinished business (something you need to resolve with your own family, parents, siblings, etc.)?

3. What do you want to know about your future spouse's family system that you haven't asked?

THREE

The balancing act called family

Louise Pyers

When we get married, we each have many spoken and unspoken expectations of what our married life will be like. It is to be hoped that we have discussed some of these dreams and goals with each other. Most couples do. We see ourselves as becoming a family, and we think about the possibilities that being a family entails.

Most couples, however, don't look at family from the perspective of being a "system." We might relate the word "system" to the solar system or a computer system or other technical areas that lend themselves to that terminology. But the family is, in fact, a system. All the parts are in some way interconnected and interdependent on one another.

A system works and functions through various patterns and roles. Each part does something to contribute to the functioning of the whole. One can compare it to a mobile: if we remove a piece, or if a piece is disturbed in any way, the entire mobile shifts and struggles to readjust until a new balance is established or the original balance is restored. This adjustment process is difficult. There is sometimes a lot of moving, shifting, and tension to find a new balance that works.

That's just how families work, too. As you create your new family as husband and wife, you will be establishing, through your roles and behaviors, your own special balance. And that balance will continually change and shift as your relationship evolves over time.

What are some of these roles and behaviors? They are patterns that occur to varying degree in most couple relationships, and we have learned most of them in our own families of origin.

We may say that when we marry we're leaving our families of origin behind "for better or for worse." Or we may plan to stay closely connected. But in either case we need to remember, "Objects in the rearview mirror are closer than they appear."

Looking at how our original families function can give us some important insights into the patterns of relating that we will most likely bring into our own marriage. We each may assume that our new family will be like our own family of origin, or we may expect it to be totally different. Whatever the case, we all carry the baggage from our original families with us. That's a given. What we do with it is up to us to decide.

So, how do we begin? What are we supposed to look for? It may help for each of us to ask ourselves the following questions about our own family of origin:

1. Who was the "distancer," the strong, silent type?

Distancers tend to be passive and laid back. They tend to be quiet or to withdraw when they need to figure something out. Distancers are models of "self-control" and tend to look at facts for information. They can be relied upon for a lot of "concrete" help doing things for other family members, but they do not see the need for a strong emotional connection. They see relationship connected more to what one does than to what one feels.

2. Who was the "pursuer"?

Pursuers sometimes place a sense of immediacy on the relationship. They need to have things done according to their own schedule. They tend to try to talk things out with someone rather than withdraw and can become over-responsible regarding the emotions of others. They are outgoing. Pursuers place much importance on being emotionally connected on a "feeling" level.

3. Who tended to overfunction?

Overfunctioners tend to want to "pick up the slack." They are the ones who will take on the responsibility for someone else, even if that person is perfectly capable. They have a hard time seeing a task that is unfinished and tend to want to take care of it themselves.

4. Who tended to underfunction?

Underfunctioners don't see the urgency in getting things done, and if someone else wants to take over certain tasks, that's fine with them. It's not that they're lazy, but if there's someone willing to pick up where they left off, so be it.

We all use the above roles and behaviors to varying degrees in our relationships, whether at work or at home. That's how we keep the balance in our lives. The key point to remember is that there can't be an underfunctioner without an overfunctioner. There can't be a distancer without a pursuer. That's how a system works. There is nothing inherently wrong with these patterns, either, if we can adapt and adjust as we seek a comfortable balance.

I have had both pursuing and distancing roles in my marital relationship. My husband has adopted both roles from time to time also. Initially our roles were pretty flexible, until our first child was born. My preoccupation with our infant son led me to overfunction in the parenting department and underfunction in the relationship with my husband. Hence I became the distancer in the relationship. He began to pursue with gusto and finally let me know that he felt left out, even though it was hard for him to admit that he felt displaced in my affections by a child he also loved very dearly.

It took some adjusting and communication about our parenting roles and our relationship to achieve finally a precarious balance. We each still have our primary operating tendency, though, and have determined that in the majority of cases I tend to pursue and my husband tends to distance. Looking back at our families of origin, we were able to find very similar patterns in how our mothers and fathers pursued and distanced in certain situations.

As another example, in our family I tend to overfunction when it comes to maintaining the family finances. My husband tends to underfunction, since he knows I will take care of it. But when I began to underfunction in this area because of other responsibilities, we had to make a major shift and do a lot of negotiating as to how to share this responsibility more equitably. It took me a while to learn not to overfunction, while it took a lot of adjustment on my husband's part to assume a little more responsibility. Why was it so difficult for us? When we looked back at our families of origin, we realized it was my mother who was in charge in the financial area and his mother who was responsible for their family finances, so we were both operating with the expectation that the woman would take care of these things.

How did members of your family seek to keep the balance when stress hit? Who was the one who needed to be in control? Who was the caretaker, the rescuer, the negotiator, or the person who always seemed to get into trouble? Who was the martyr, the hero, the goody two-shoes? What roles did you play? The patterns we saw and the roles we ourselves played in our family of origin are the ones we will most likely repeat in our own marriage. No one is immune to these patterns and roles. They are just there.

All families are messy. No family is perfect. This scrambling for balance is a constant dynamic in all families, and distinct patterns of relating are there. We just have to take the time to look at them.

In some families members get stuck into one or two patterns of relating. Their system is rigid. Members have more difficulty bouncing from one role to another and are more or less forced to adapt to one or two roles. This type of family becomes increasingly dysfunctional since the options for adapting to different situations are limited.

In such a family, one's way of perceiving the world becomes tunnel vision. Thinking becomes distorted because of limitations imposed by unspoken rules in the family, such as:

1. Don't talk.
Don't discuss this problem and maybe it will go away.

2. Don't trust.
Don't trust your perception because we'll tell you you're wrong. For instance, "Daddy's not drunk, he's just tired."

3. Don't feel.
Don't feel that way. Don't be angry. Don't be sad.

The point is that all families have spoken or unspoken rules, especially when in stressful situations. This is a constant process, and it is necessary to keep our eyes open and look for and be aware of these patterns throughout our lives. And it helps to use our rearview mirror, for that rearview mirror can help us to look at where we've been. It can also help us see that as individuals we do not operate in a vacuum.

Everything we do has an effect on other people in the family systems in which we operate. What other people do always affects us. The mobile is constantly moving, adjusting. Every relationship, be it marriage, work, or friendship, is another string connected to our family-of-origin mobile. For that is where we first learned about love, trust, and how to relate to others. We apply what we learned there to all of our other relationships. Our original families provide us with our own unique lens with which we see and interact in our world.

The balancing act called family is all part of knowing who we are and where we came from. It is extremely important, however, not to blame others or to excuse ourselves by saying, "Well, that's just the way I am." We have to take responsibility for our own actions. If the patterns we inherited aren't good for our new family, it's our responsibility—working as a couple—to change them.

DISCUSSION QUESTIONS

1.   As you look at your family of origin, what role or roles did you take on most consistently? How did it serve you? How did it serve your family?

2.   As you look at your new relationship, what role or roles have you already taken on? How does it serve you? How does it serve the relationship?

3.   Remembering that change is necessary for growth, is there room in your new family for a change of roles? Would it be good for you both? Why or why not?

FOUR

Assumptions in marriage

Patrick Brennan

Couples bring certain "assumptions" into marriage on their wedding day, most of which relate to how they expect their future spouse to act once the wedding gifts are put away.

Dr. David Thomas of Regis College in Denver, Colorado, has studied the "real issues" behind the most common assumptions and how marital communication is the only way to keep these expectations from being a negative influence on the relationship.

Dr. Thomas, director of the graduate program in Adult Christian Community Development at Regis, is a lay theologian, lecturer, and author of numerous books, articles, and papers on marriage and family and the connections between religion and contemporary life. He was an adviser to the U.S. Bishops' delegation to the World Synod on Family in 1980.

He and his wife, Karen, have been married twenty-two years and have five children, three of whom are presently in college. They have been foster parents for more than fifty children, primarily babies and toddlers.

Dr. Thomas notes that "assumptions are unproven statements or thoughts about the way things are," and that "if you assume, you've got problems."

Engaged couples should realize, he says, that "you marry not only a person, you marry a family. Your partner's family brings all sorts of things into your marriage."

Dr. Thomas has identified the issues behind ten common assumptions in marriage:

1. **I can change you:**
   This is a definite "false assumption." "If you want to change something in your marriage," Dr. Thomas says, "you must change yourself — you can't change the other person." You are usually attracted to another person because either they have qualities similar to yours, or they have qualities that you yourself lack. To try to change those qualities after the wedding is both unfair and counterproductive.

2. **We'll live happily ever after:**
   This notion of marriage, Dr. Thomas explains, has its roots in thirteenth century "fatalism" that gave rise to the "myth of romantic love." He notes that contrary to this assumption, "Marriage starts something, it doesn't end something."

   Marriage has its good and bad moments, its romantic and dry spells. "Love is an act of the will," he states. "There are at least two times you marry your spouse: once, when you take your vows on your wedding day, and again, when you move to a more mature love."

   Speaking of when this "move" takes place, Dr. Thomas points out that work and children are challenging aspects of the process. There is a constant forming and re-forming of the relationship taking place, he says. "Don't be afraid of crisis points in marriage," he explains. "They are movements toward a deeper love."

   Other things affecting the move to a mature love, he states, are unexpected expenses and a job loss. "Economics have a major impact," he says. "That marriages are coming at a later age is directly related to economics." Often too, a spouse will blame the other for an economic problem such as a job loss or money problems, when in reality the cause of the stress is beyond the control of either spouse.

   The Baby Boom generation was subjected to a massive amount of advertising that told them the good life was their right, Dr. Thomas notes. The problem is that the U.S. economy has changed and children may not even reach the same standard of living their parents enjoy, let alone exceed it.

3. **Nothing will ever change:**

   "If you're not changing, you're dead," Dr. Thomas asserts. "The process of growth and change goes on throughout life. Things are always changing, hopefully for the better."

4. **We'll raise our kids the right way:**

   Statistics bear out that couples will repeat the parenting style of their own parents, unless they are consciously aware of it and try to change. "Ask yourself how you were parented," Dr. Thomas suggests. He adds that couples should not worry excessively if they don't agree totally on parenting styles, as the children will benefit from the variety to which they're subjected.

5. **We're in charge; we'll make the decisions:**

   "Young couples like to think that now that they're married, they're in their own little world," Dr. Thomas points out. "The reality is that most decisions are still made for us by employers, parents, and Mother Nature."

6. **Marriage solves problems:**

   "If only we were married, then everything would be fine," is a common lament of the dating or engaged couple encountering problems. "Marriage doesn't solve all problems," Dr. Thomas says, "rather, it creates them."

   He describes the differences in attitude toward marriage between older couples and younger couples getting married: Older couples tend to be more realistic about the challenges facing them in marriage. They may be more independent of one another if they have lived alone for a long period of time. They're not usually "moonstruck" with each other. On the other hand, they may be more cynical towards marriage than younger couples.

7. **In sexuality, practice makes perfect:**

   This is an attitude that underlies some couples' decision to live together before marriage. "They say they don't want to repeat the mistakes of their parents," Dr. Thomas explains, "and view pre-marital sex as a test for compatibility." Yet he notes that studies done on the effect of a couple living together before marriage have all come to the conclusion that it has "zero effect" on guaranteeing a happy marriage or preventing a divorce later on.

"Living together before marriage only helps you find out that you can or cannot live together before marriage," Dr. Thomas states simply.

8. My spouse is perfect; I am not:
"We tend to glorify our spouse, usually because we tended to glorify our parents," Dr. Thomas maintains. "This comes from dealing with the lack of perfection in our parents. That is, if one or both of the parents exhibited behavior unacceptable to the child, rather than admit that the parent was not perfect the child 'flip-flopped' and concluded, 'I am not perfect.'"

9. Two make one:
Contrary to modern thought, Dr. Thomas contends, male and female are very different in how they approach relationships, commitments, and problem-solving. Despite being married, you will always remain two individuals of the opposite sex.

10. When it gets tough, we'll split:
"There can't be a young person today who hasn't had experience with divorce among relatives or friends," Dr. Thomas notes. Yet Christian marriage is still a lifetime commitment. "Don't compare your marriage to others as a measure of its success," he urges. "And don't neglect forming a couple spirituality. God has an investment in you as a married couple."

Marital communication, Dr. Thomas concludes, is the actual testing out of any assumptions brought into the relationship through marriage. He reminds couples that at its core, marriage was intended to engender generosity and altruism as it forces one to become less self-centered by having to deal intimately with another.

"Marriage was designed to give us the opportunity to 'get out of ourselves,' " he declares. "God knew what he was doing."

DISCUSSION QUESTIONS:

1. Which of the ten assumptions discussed in this article do you wish you could prove true? Why? Where did you first learn this assumption? From whom? What are your feelings when you imagine yourself letting go of it?

2. What assumptions do you think your partner may be harboring? Talk about them.

3. How does marriage give you the opportunity to "get out of yourselves"?

FIVE

The Engaged Encounter Weekend

Ralph and JoAnn Taft

With schedules that are more tightly packed than sardines, most of us — single, married, or engaged — are not looking for one more commitment. We all experience the defeat of trying to arrange a little free time, only to find these free dates fill up with appointments.

Believe it or not, taking time out for an Engaged Encounter Weekend with your future spouse will not add to your already hectic lifestyles, but rather will help you cope with the busy schedules, stress, and pressures of your new life together.

Planning for a wedding is chaotic at times, but it need not pull us apart from each other. If we find ourselves arguing about wedding plans, schedules, appointments, and family feuds, perhaps what we really need to do is to get away from it all to reflect on what is happening to us as individuals and as a couple.

As a volunteer "presenting" couple on the Engaged Encounter Weekend, the two most common questions we hear from couples is whether Engaged Encounter is a retreat and whether it's just for Catholics. Some also express hesitation because they feel that someone is trying to corner them into another "holy roller" event sponsored by the Catholic Church.

Yes, it is a retreat in the sense that we leave the "outside world" and our normal routine for the duration of the weekend. And although the weekend can be part of the marriage preparation required in order for a wedding to be held in a Catholic church, all couples are welcome no matter what their religious beliefs. No one will coerce anyone to become a Catholic on an Engaged Encounter Weekend. If the weekend is considered "holy," it's holy in the sense of being real, enjoyable, and having the potential to add a deeper dimension to the relationship a couple already shares.

We can still recall our own hesitation, thirteen years ago, when we were preparing for our wedding by meeting with a married couple. Our reaction was very defensive: "No one could tell us what our marriage is going to be like when they didn't even know us!" It's probably safe to say that some engaged couples — like us back then — initially participate in an Engaged Encounter Weekend to satisfy a Church obligation and get it over with. What they invariably leave with, however, is a closer bond and a deeper sense of commitment to each other.

Some might ask, "Is all this marriage preparation really necessary, or is it just another formality of the Church?" That might best be answered after one participates in an Engaged Encounter. When couples experience the Church as an active group of people rather than a passive building, their questions and hesitation gradually fade away.

Engaged Encounter is not a weekend of "teaching and preaching," but rather of sharing — privately as a couple. A progressive series of talks is presented, and each engaged couple is then invited to write their responses to discussion questions on the topic and discuss them together.

The two couples and priest who make up the presenting team are not paid to be there — they volunteer. Why? Because they believe in marriage and want to share their everyday experiences — good and bad — in order to help the engaged couples present come to a deeper understanding of marriage.

The benefits of participating in an Engaged Encounter Weekend can perhaps best be explained by sharing the unfolding beauty of a rosebud: Nothing can hurry a rose to open. We cannot coax it any faster. Each day it is beautiful in itself as each petal opens itself to the final beauty of a flower in full bloom. Likewise, on an Engaged Encounter Weekend, no one will put any pressure on attending couples, and they will not be graded on their participation. Participants unfold quietly and uniquely as the weekend progresses until their own inner beauty is fully apparent to their partners.

We invite you to attend such a weekend, to come away from that hectic time before the wedding and give each other the gift of quality time and love! Check with your parish priest or diocesan Family Life Office for weekend dates and registration information.

DISCUSSION QUESTIONS:

1. How much time have you set aside to look at your relationship as compared to time preparing for the wedding, the reception, and so forth?

2. How do you feel about having time and space with your future spouse to share, to allow your "inner self" to become apparent? What resources do you need to make that happen?

3. Should you make an Engaged Encounter Weekend? When?

SIX

Big wedding or small wedding?

Donald and Christine Paglia

Jan and Bob are getting married in seven months and are planning a very large wedding. They have hired a six-piece band. There will be five bridesmaids and ushers in the wedding party, plus a ring bearer and flower girl. They have invited three hundred guests and the reception will take place at the country club with all the stops pulled out. Jan's and Bob's parents have taken out small loans to pay many of the costs.

Ted and Louise are to be married in four months. They are getting married in Louise's small parish church. The wedding reception will take place in her parents' back yard. The meal will be a covered-dish affair. The wedding cake is being made by the bride's uncle. They will have taped music for dancing. The bride and groom have asked that the guests bring only a basket of non-perishables to be donated to a local soup kitchen.

These two scenarios are about as different as can be. They represent the two ends of the spectrum of wedding plans and viewpoints. Often, people have strong feelings as to which choice is the correct one from a Christian perspective. Each of these two different approaches to celebrating Christian marriage do similar things, and within each approach there can be found a piece of wisdom that can help to serve the very purpose of a wedding celebration.

At the wedding feast at Cana recorded in John's Gospel, Jesus first revealed himself. He did so at the request of his mother, Mary. Mary had become so concerned that the bridal party not be embarrassed by the lack of wine that she asked Jesus for a miracle. Jesus complied.

It is not known exactly how long this wedding feast went on, but it is safe to say that because of Mary and Jesus the party lasted a bit longer than it might have. During Jesus' time, wedding feasts commonly lasted for three days; a full week if the family was wealthy. People needed to travel long distances by horse, mule, or carriage. They would have to be put up overnight for the length of the party. It was a true community event, one that the entire village might be involved in preparing for and participating in. The Jews used the occasion as a time to celebrate life, particularly marriage and family life. It was a time of ritual, meaning, and celebration.

Usually we think of God being revealed at the wedding Mass. By revealing himself at the wedding feast at Cana two thousand years ago, however, Jesus made the entire wedding feast sacramental. That is, the feast itself was important enough to Jesus for him to change water into wine so that the participants could continue to celebrate what God considered a sacred union. Two people, proclaiming their love for one another through their wedding celebration, is a clear, palpable sign of God's love.

On the one hand, however, couples can have a large and lavish reception that is not a holy experience. The bigness can smother the actual meaning of the event. On the other hand, couples can also have a small and rigid reception that is so restrictive that the celebration aspect is all but lost. Both meaning and celebration need to be attended to. The couple cannot afford to lose sight of either.

In trying to express the meaning of the wedding reception, the couple needs to ask themselves questions: What are we trying to convey by this wedding feast? Can it be sacramental — that is, how will it embody God's presence? How will our reception symbolize the deeper meaning of life itself? How will Jesus be revealed in the food or drink at our reception? Is God's generosity made apparent through this feast?

As to celebration, attention needs to be placed on the kind of space and time for the wedding reception. Again, there are questions the couple needs to address: Who is the celebration for? The couple? Parents? The guests? Does this reception celebration express who we are and who we want to become as a couple?

The couple can create a wedding reception that is really a continuation of the liturgy begun at the church with Mass. The liturgy of the reception can be holy; holy, but not dull. The physical arrangements can speak to the sense of joy and celebration. The bountiful foods and the dancing can express the sacredness and awesomeness of God's creation. Like the wedding liturgy, the wedding reception can be a tremendous encounter with God's incredible love for us. It is certainly a time of joy, a time to stop the ordinary work of daily life and instead use play as a way to be touched and deepened in the sense of God's presence.

The wedding reception of the Christian couple must be countercultural. That is, it must be different from the way society operates on any given day. It must be opposed to the way society worships consumerism and materialism, by expressing a God-centered joy about life itself. The couple that has the fancy, elaborate wedding, if done so because the couple wishes to glorify their God's generosity, can create a countercultural moment of grace. If they are having the super-extravaganza merely to impress others, however, they are possibly guilty of worshipping a false god. The couple who diminish the reception celebration because they reject the notion of joy and celebration, on the other hand, deny themselves the opportunity to witness that their God is extravagant. If they restrict the feast in such a way as to acknowledge that those who have been given much are also responsible to give to those who have little, however, then they are serving the same God that has blessed them with each other and with life.

Perhaps a third case can illustrate a movement toward more meaningful and more celebrative wedding plans.

Karen and Steve are both involved in planning their wedding. They intend to meet their friends and guests as they arrive at the church. The bride and groom will process together up the aisle with both sets of parents. They have planned to have the reception at their parish community center. The entire parish of about two hundred and fifty has been invited to attend. They have hired a caterer and have supplemented the meal with special dishes from their respective Italian and Polish backgrounds. A group of musician friends will play music to reflect the heritage of both families. Members of their wedding party purchased a new outfit (a new suit for the men and a moderately priced dress that is versatile for the women) instead of renting. They plan to donate ten percent of their wedding gifts to a favorite charity. Photos of themselves and of family members and friends, both alive and deceased, will be arranged at the hall for their guests to see. They have eliminated the head table and plan to interact with their guests by moving around to each table throughout the celebration.

Often we in family ministry ask a couple not to spend so much time focusing on the wedding and instead spend time on preparing for their marriage. It is possible, however, for couples to give serious consideration to their wedding and reception and by so doing end up focusing on the values underlying their marriage. If a couple looks at the wedding and reception as a sacred ritual, they can find in it a kaleidoscope of their very relationship.

DISCUSSION QUESTIONS:

1. God is love, and the one who abides in love abides in God. How has love (God) been revealed to you as a couple? Is there a symbol or image that captures some of that meaning for you? How could that symbol or image be used in your wedding celebration?

2. What does the phrase "countercultural" mean to you in the context of a wedding celebration? How could it be true for you in your wedding?

3. For the interfaith couple: How can aspects of both of your faith traditions be acknowledged and affirmed in your wedding celebration?

seven

Making social justice a welcome wedding guest

Father Thomas Bennett

"My Godmother will bring up the hosts, Father, and Jean's Godmother will bring up the wine, and my Godfather will bring up a fruit basket, if that's all right."

"Sure, Mike, that'll be fine."

The Catholic book store had sent us a new supply of Father Joseph Champlin's perennial guide for the engaged, *Together for Life*. I noted that the cover was different, but surely nothing else had changed. I could tell that by flipping through the pages. Well, I was almost right. There was one small, subtle, and yet significant change. On the sheet that the couple fills out with their selections of readings and prayers, they are asked to specify who will bring forward the gifts at the presentation and then are asked if they wish to make a symbolic gift for the poor.

A symbolic gift for the poor? When two people are so very much in love, their love focuses on each other, but that love also needs to reach out to others. What better time than at a wedding to present a symbolic gift for the poor? Marriage is a time of symbols—the rings, the cake, the bouquet, indeed, even the garter. Something old, something new, something borrowed, something blue.

I am not one to add new symbols to the liturgy easily. When "wedding candles" were popular a few years ago, I thought that we had enough symbols, and to add what seemed to me to be a weak and ambiguous one was not in the best interest of the clarity and strength of our liturgy. You can't blame the candle companies for trying. After all, Hallmark has brought us Grandparents' Day, and FTD florists presents us with Secretaries' Day.

Then why am I so excited about the new symbolic gift for the poor? Because it symbolizes our basic commitment to Jesus' preferential love for the poor; because it goes to the heart of the couple's "becoming a sacrament"— their love a sign of God's love; because it symbolizes a rich commitment and a depth of love.

The words of the final blessing at the marriage ceremony are, to me, so full of hope: "May you always bear witness to the love of God in this world so that the afflicted and needy will find in you generous friends and welcome you into the joys of heaven."

Years ago, when I was first ordained, a priest friend told me about a suggestion he made to couples as they prepared for marriage. He would discuss with them their love as a sign of Christ's love and discuss Christ's love for the poor. He would speak of our Western civilization in which the symbols of our very existence are our time and our money (oh, how we guard our time even more than our money!).

My priest friend would suggest to the couple that as part of their wedding they agree to spend "a significant amount of their time" and "a significant amount of their money" in doing something special for the poor. He would further suggest that each year on their wedding anniversary they make a new commitment to spend a significant amount of their time and money reaching out to the poor.

For each couple the significant amount of time or money would be different. From year to year what is significant would change. The key was to be specific. Imagine Mike and Jean on their twenty-fifth wedding anniversary, looking back and looking forward. Imagine Jean saying, "Remember your Godfather bringing up that basket of fruit and all the people at the reception wondering what that was all about?" Picture them as they remember what they did each year. Remember with them the years when money was tight and their time was stretched. Remember with them the years when things were easier and they could do more. Remember with them twenty-five specific commitments of time and money to the poor.

Remember with them as well who "the poor" were each year. On their sixth anniversary the poor were Mike's grandparents. His grandfather died three weeks after their anniversary. Remember with them how happy they were that they had packed the kids in the car and gone to Syracuse to see him before he died. Remember with them their third anniversary when they were still living in the apartment and the landlord had broken his pelvis and was out of work for so long. Remember the meals that they had made for him, and the rides to the doctor, and the long waits in his office.

Then there was the year they volunteered the six Tuesday evenings in a row at Hospice; and the one when the peewee soccer league was two coaches short and Mike's team beat Jean's team; and the year of the exchange student and how homesick she was. Remember with them the years when they discussed for days what to do for that year's anniversary project for the poor and how they had to be very creative; and remember the years when there was but one choice—so clear a need and so great an opportunity.

"So that the afflicted and needy will find in you generous friends," says the wedding prayer. Who are the afflicted and needy? Who are the poor, who is my neighbor? There is but one answer: "I was hungry and you gave me to eat, I was thirsty and you gave me to drink, I was homeless and you took me in, I was naked and you clothed me."

The wedding prayer continues, "Father, you have made the bond of marriage a holy mystery, a symbol of Christ's love for his Church. Hear our prayers for Mike and Jean. With faith in you and in each other, they pledge their love today. May their lives always bear witness to the reality of that love. We ask you this through our Lord Jesus Christ, your Son, who lives and reigns with you and the Holy Spirit, one God, for ever and ever. Amen."

DISCUSSION QUESTIONS:

1. What memories do you have from your family of origin of sharing time/money with the poor? Who were the afflicted and needy in your own surroundings growing up?

2. Your love is a sign of God's love in the world. How could you envision yourselves expressing that love for the poor, the afflicted, the needy? What could keep you from expressing that love?

3. What are you doing now—as individuals or as a couple — to help others? Is there one project you could do together before your wedding?

EIGHT

Sex, marriage, and the Catholic Church

Dr. Thomas and Donna Finn

"Oh, yes, yes. . . more, more, up just a little higher, Honey, oh, that's just right."

And with that, the kitchen clock was finally hung.

When talking about sex, it is very easy for us to connect various expectations, opinions, or feelings to particular aspects of sexuality. In reading the opening sentence, for example, it is quite likely that the picture in our mind was one of heated romance rather than hanging a clock.

Similarly, when we used to hear the words "sex" and "Catholic Church" in the same discussion, we tended to associate words like "oppressive," "guilt," "rigid," and "puritanical" in describing the relationship between them.

Over our ten years of marriage, however, our sexual joys and struggles have made the meaning of sex in a Catholic/Christian context come alive for us in ways that have been enriching, fulfilling, fun, and challenging.

One of the first struggles we had was dealing with our mutually and firmly held belief that the Catholic Church (indeed, God) taught that sexual intercourse was something couples did to have children — a lot of them. In contrast to secular society's message that sex was fun and carefree, this one wasn't exactly thrilling.

Luckily, we came to realize that we were missing the boat. We learned that God and our Church view sex in marriage not as a duty but as the most powerful and intimate way in which we tell one another how deeply in love we are. It is passionate, gentle, exciting, fun, and brings into focus our willingness to give each other the most personal thing we can — our bodies — in a way that is unconditional and mutually caring. Indeed, when we share ourselves in intercourse, we are mirroring God's desire to love us in a way that is unconditional and mutually caring.

A second struggle in putting together "sex" and "Church" was in the area of birth control. Prior to our wedding, we did a lot of exploring of different artificial birth control methods and were not comfortable with any of them because of their side effects or just the nature of the methods themselves. Also, we knew the Church says we shouldn't use artificial methods, so you can imagine our anxiety as we looked at using the old "rhythm" method. We wanted to have children, but not right away, and felt quite relieved when we learned of the method called Natural Family Planning (NFP).

NFP is the process of identifying the fertile time in a woman's cycle through the changes in bodily symptoms of temperature, cervical mucus, cervical texture and position, and then choosing not to have intercourse during those fertile times.

NFP is as effective as the best artificial methods, but on top of that it has contributed greatly to enhancing our sex lives since it requires mutual communication, mutual responsibility for sexual decisions, self-awareness, self-control, and a willingness never to take sex and/or each other for granted.

Additionally, using NFP has enriched our sexual relationship, as it has put us more in touch and in tune with each other. It has allowed us to keep intercourse natural and in harmony with God's plan for sex, that is, not to alter purposefully the way God physically created us or to prevent by artificial means the possibility of a child's being conceived.

One of our greatest joys has been the ability to conceive each of our children using Natural Family Planning. Since we could identify our fertile days, we knew that the sharing of our love in intercourse on those days could result in a child's birth, and we truly felt God's creative presence and a partnership with God in creating new life during those times. We know that if it was not for our Church's teachings on human sexuality, we never would have understood the true meaning and power of our sexual love.

Talking openly about our sexual concerns has also been aided by our use of NFP. Since it requires good communication, it has been helpful in dealing with the different sexual expectations that we each brought to our relationship. Although we can still struggle with these issues, we have a vehicle for working them through. I (Tom), for example, had a belief that the frequency of sex represented the degree of love Donna had for me and often felt hurt and rejected when our schedules did not permit much sexual intimacy. Through discussion, sharing, and exploration, I've been able to see that my "sex equals love" connection was nothing but self-defeating, and I have become more confident in Donna's unconditional acceptance of me. Again, I can see how our Church's sexual values have allowed me to experience a greater depth of love for Donna, myself, and God.

Another joy and challenge for us has been not to limit our expression of love to sexual intercourse alone. When we support each other in household activities, listen to each other's job ups and downs, call one another to just say "hi," leave love notes, hug, and hold hands, we demonstrate our promise to love.

Our commitment to build and nurture our relationship is fed by this type of twenty-four hour love relationship. The physical love we share, then, becomes more fulfilling as it fits into our overall relationship and becomes an affirmation of our marriage commitment.

As we learn more and more about the Catholic Church's teachings on human sexuality, and as our sexual relationship continues to evolve with new challenges (such as a three-year-old yelling, "I have to go potty," in the middle of a passionate evening encounter!), we are confident that we will come to an even greater appreciation of the love we have for each other. Sometimes new understanding comes to us unexpectedly; other times we have to seek it out.

Either way, our goal is to stay open to God's plan for us in the context of our sexual love, as we know there is great wisdom and happiness in it.

Our hope is that other couples will find the same joy that we have found in our journey and that their marriage too can find root in God's unceasing love.

We pray also that as the months and years move on, and you hear the words "sex" and "Church" in the same context, rather than say to yourselves, "Oh, no," you might say instead, "Yes, yes. More, more."

DISCUSSION QUESTIONS:

1. What are some presumptions, beliefs, and so forth, that you carry around in your head when you hear "sex and the Catholic Church"?

2. What would be some barriers which prevent you from trusting the Catholic Church's view of sex and marriage?

3. What are your feelings about having and spacing children in your upcoming marriage?

NINE

Natural Family Planning — what is it?

Jeanne Brenia, R.N.

God made men to be physically fertile generally all of the time; and God made women to be physically fertile only some of the time. Natural Family Planning (NFP) is a way married couples can live in harmony with the way God created us.

Women have been given certain natural body indicators to determine when they are fertile. Natural Family Planning is a means of learning how to interpret these signs of fertility. Relying on NFP can express a faith that the laws of nature were designed by God for a divine purpose.

Once a couple has learned to recognize the fertile and infertile signs, they can use this information either to plan or to avoid pregnancy. Those who wish to prevent conception would abstain from intercourse during the fertile time. Couples who seek to achieve pregnancy would be able to enhance their chances by knowing when the woman is most fertile.

One of the woman's bodily signs of fertility is a changing pattern of vaginal secretions produced in the cervix of the uterus. Another signal that ovulation has occurred is a sustained rise in body temperature. Couples can rely on one or both of these indicators to identify the fertile days of each menstrual cycle. Some women find that additional physical signs are helpful indicators too, such as a particular pain or heaviness in the abdomen or pelvic area or changes in the cervix itself.

On a daily basis, the woman takes her waking temperature and notices the absence or presence of a cervical mucous discharge from the vagina. She may also observe some of the other supportive signs related to ovulation. These observations and the temperature are noted on a simple chart.

Her husband may be involved in some of this process, as well as in the interpretation of these signs. This is meant to be a cooperative method, not just because the postponement of intercourse affects both of them, but also because it is more effective if they share in the responsibility and decision-making.

So, how effective is it? Natural Family Planning has been studied by various organizations around the world, including our own government. When used correctly, NFP is 98 to 99 percent effective.

Natural Family Planning is not the same as the Calendar-Rhythm Method. That method was established on the assumption that a woman could have predictable times of fertility and infertility based on the lengths of her past menstrual cycles. Since many women occasionally have irregular cycles, the predictions were sometimes wrong.

Women can have irregular cycles and still use NFP successfully, because the changes are observed as they occur in each individual menstrual cycle.

The use of Natural Family Planning has many advantages. There is a greater awareness of our fertility as part of the normal, healthy way our bodies work. We can be more attuned to the ways our cycles affect the way we feel.

NFP is safe and natural, with no risks to health or our future ability to conceive a child. It encourages self-reliance, is economical, and can be used throughout a woman's child-bearing years.

The times of abstinence can be used as a motivation to rely on other signs of caring to nurture the relationship. This can enhance the appreciation of each other when the infertile time arrives. NFP gives us a chance to practice receptivity, patience, and self-control, all very important to marriage itself.

It should be acknowledged that NFP asks more of the couple than other types of family planning. Periodic abstinence can be very challenging and requires the commitment of both husband and wife. Careful attentiveness and a creative response are needed for NFP to work well in both family planning and marriage enrichment.

NFP is not just an alternative birth control method. It is built on an appreciation of our fertility and sexuality as precious gifts to be used wisely. We are enabled to connect our actions more directly with their natural consequences. Above all, however, we need God's help in using these gifts to serve his will.

NFP cannot be learned just by reading about it. It takes time and education by someone professionally trained in the method to be used properly and effectively. To attend classes, contact your local Catholic hospital or a Catholic diocesan agency such as its Family Life Office.

DISCUSSION QUESTIONS:

1. Do you pay attention to your own body? When? Why?

2. Could your bodies be spiritual as well as physical guides to your relationship? If yes, how could that be? If not, why not?

3. What do you think about using Natural Family Planning in your marriage?

TEN

Marriage as a sacrament

Father Patrick Berkery

When I first became interested in the sacramental dimension of marriage, I was baffled by the divorce statistics. I became aware of the fact that many marriages were not working. The split-ups, the extra-marital affairs, the resulting pain and heartache shouted that somehow we priests were not offering the proper preparation for marriage. For example, I heard more and more young people tell me they'd never tie the knot. "What for?" one girl asked. "Everyone knows that marriage is a dated concept. All it is is a piece of paper."

And so I went back to the drawing board. I spoke with my brother priests and together we reviewed the preparatory steps — the sacramental guidelines — for marriage. I also interviewed people who had been happily married over a period of time. As a result, I realized we were not presenting the entity of marriage for what it really is, that is, a *sacrament* wherein a couple live a life centered in the Lord. We weren't telling the engaged couples that in marriage each spouse should be a sacrament to the other — that is, a sign of Christ's love and his presence.

Today I stress the fact that the sacrament of marriage is not magic. A loving union doesn't automatically come with it. Partners have to blend their lives into something that is greater than both of them.

One couple told me they were still together because of this realization. "If we couldn't create more than ourselves, we'd each be the loser," they said.

The fact is, each couple needs to create a unity that signals God's love to each other and the world. By marrying in the Church we are saying to our spiritual community that we want the spiritual aspects of our marriage to grow and flourish. Thus we commit to each other and to God to make this happen. This is what I mean by the sacramental dimension of marriage. It is a specific and effective spiritual sign.

The way to foster and nurture marriage so that it is a sign of God's love to each partner and the world is through sharing. *Marriage is a lifetime of sharing, understanding, accepting, and loving each other. It is not an escape from, but a step to, a new life.*

One older couple I know understands this quite well, and practices it by constantly attempting to "walk in the other's shoes." They don't begin decision-making or choice selection by trying to get the better of each other.

"How do you avoid manipulation?" I asked. They both smiled and said that they knew each other so well they could read each other's mind. But that's never their starting point. As the wife put it, "We try to tell each other the truth every time. The truth is greater than us both."

So what do married couples share? I think you must share holistically, that is, through the body, mind, and spirit. You do this best if you are willing to open up and exchange three things:

1. **values,**

2. **the self,**

3. **respect.**

First of all it is important to realize that values cannot be overlooked in marriage. Why? Because values are personal criteria of worth that guide our every choice. Values make up our attitude, that core of beliefs that guide us in the choices we make every day. If someone or something doesn't meet our value system's demands, we bypass it, ignore it, or reject it.

We create our daily routines based on our conscious or unconscious values. This is important to understand if we are serious about sharing our routine with another on an intimate level.

Studies indicate that values between those who are engaged need not be identical, but unless each person's values are revealed, discussed, and shared, couples end up taking each other for granted. Furthermore, engaged couples need to realize that at this point in their lives they are not seeking conversion of the other at the value level. Different values can enhance the health of any relationship.

For example, if we insist that "my way is best," that "I am the intellectual," or that "you are too 'artsy,' " then we close off any opportunity to benefit from the riches the other person's value system can provide. The truth is that few values are absolute. We all see the world from our own unique perspective. We each come from a different heritage, ethnic background, tradition, and family history. These need to be named and honored as tools with which to learn more about each other. They help a couple understand how each partner views the world.

I believe that most marriages fail because the authenticity of the other's values is ignored. The most opportune time to share values, explore differences, and accept their authenticity is before you walk down the aisle. You can't share values, however, if you don't even realize their import and impact on the subsequent relationship.

Critics argue that values are expendable if the couple loves each other. It's the old saw, "If you really loved me, you would. . . ." My response is that you can't barter values, because values are to a person what the nucleus is to the cell. Values are that basic.

However, the sacramentality of marriage is upheld when couples not only share their *values* with each other but are willing to share their total *selves* through communication. Authentic communication gives meaning to and preserves the sacramental dimension of marriage. Any sacrament is a sign. A sign is a directive, telling something about something other than itself.

My friend Sean thought he knew all about signs and communication. After all, he taught speech at the local community college. But one day he was reading scripture and chose to meditate on what he called a "worn-out text." The text was, "In the beginning was the Word and the Word was with God."

Well, he did learn something, Sean said. "I ran home and admitted to my wife that I had been struggling with the meaning of the word "communication" and what it meant to us. I shared with her that I had finally come to the conclusion that real communication is not just a word, it's the person revealed behind the word." He went on to say that if they could learn to truly see and sense each other's self in their daily words together, their level of communication would become more spiritual, more dynamic, more effective. And time proved him right.

It is vital to realize that communication is more than simple small talk. It is more than expressing one's opinion as to what brand of paper towels is the better "picker-upper." Communication, to be meaningful, must center on in-depth matters which can deepen love.

Communication means sharing feelings. That means partners do not hide behind pouting, sarcasm, or belittling. In other words, the mature couple shares their anger, their hurts, their dreams, their disappointments. They do not manipulate through immature withholding of kindness and love in order to get even.

When they share themselves through honest communication, however, they are constantly rediscovering each other. The sensitive communicator in marriage is alert to the moods, feelings, and hang-ups of the other. This mutual sharing allows for learning and for understanding. And it is here that the sign value of the sacrament of marriage flourishes.

Finally, the couple who is serious about energizing their union through the sacramental dynamism of marriage insists on mutual respect, sharing this respect at every possible moment. I know a middle-aged couple who really have a relationship of mutual respect. In fact, the first time I had dinner at their home, I was rather taken aback by the way they treated each other. Sure they teased, they laughed, they kidded. But you could almost touch the awe that thrived between them.

They weren't stuffy or plastic in any way. But when she spoke, he looked at her and gave his undivided attention. The same happened when he had something to say. They never took each other for granted. Their compliments of each other were sincere, and you knew right away that they meant what they said. Their three children were equally respectful of each other and their parents.

Such respect allows for affirmation. Without mutual respect, there is no room for the sustaining power that tells the other he or she is the greatest gift you have ever received. Affirmation, that is, naming the gift, is daily proof that a married couple are signs or sacraments to each other.

A sacramental approach also extends a couple's concerns and interests beyond themselves. The awareness that two individuals become a sacrament to each other stretches their world view so they appreciate that their marriage is not just to satisfy their own needs. Christian marriage also has a social dimension. Sacramental awareness leads the couple to go beyond themselves—sharing their love with the community, the parish, and the neighborhood in various dimensions of social justice.

Imagine how your union would be strengthened and solidified by such a holistic sharing of all you are and can be. Remember, Christian marriage has not been tried and found wanting. All too often, it has just never been tried. That is what the challenge of marriage as a sacrament offers you—now and forever.

DISCUSSION QUESTIONS:

1. What has been your experience of sharing your values with your partner? What was positive? What was negative?

2. What has been your experience of sharing yourself with your partner? What was positive? What was negative?

3. What has been your experience of sharing respect with your partner? What was positive? What was negative?

Finishing Touches

ELEVEN

Two faiths, one marriage

Father Thomas Bennett

"I'm a Lutheran, Father, and Patty is your parishioner." It sounded like an introduction to something to which this young man expected some objections from me. I remained silent and listened.

He continued, "We have been talking and would like to have my pastor take part in our wedding ceremony, perhaps read a lesson, and perhaps preach." He paused again as if he expected an interruption. I continued to listen silently.

"It is really important to us . . . and it would be important to my family. . . ." I finally broke in to ease his discomfort.

"Of course it is all right with me, Bill. In fact, if you had not mentioned it, I would have suggested it. Pastor Johnson and I have done many weddings together both here and at your church, and it works out very nicely."

Seldom have I seen two people relax so quickly and completely. They had expected to get "a hard time" and had geared themselves up for that. Obviously, they had not talked with Pastor Johnson yet or they would have known that they were far from blazing new trails in ecumenism. My mind was wandering as I thought how nice it was that I did not have to say no to something that this young couple had their hearts set upon.

I came back to reality as Patty gave a nervous laugh and said, "We were worried about this . . . I guess we should have known that you and Pastor Johnson would be comfortable praying together." She gave that nervous laugh again.

I very often say what pops into my mind without thinking it through, and this was one of those times. "Sure, Pastor Johnson and I are comfortable praying together, Patty. Are you and Bill?"

They looked at each other, they looked at me, and they looked at each other again. A tear welled up in Patty's eye, and Bill squeezed her hand. I don't recall ever having seen two people with exactly that same look before. They had my full attention now. Very calmly, Bill said to Patty, in what was a cross between a question and a statement, "It's all right to tell him?" She nodded.

I make it a practice never to meet with a couple for more than an hour at a time. That day I violated my own custom as I sat listening to their enthusiasm.

"It all started when we were discussing whether to get pre-engaged," Patty explained. The term "pre-engaged" made them both smile, as people do at a private joke. I got the impression that the use of the term was in some way a light mockery of themselves. The story, however, was far from a mockery of anything, and in fact was one of the most beautiful I have ever heard.

Bill had been an altar server in the Lutheran Church during his high school years. He had grown to become a lector. His family were churchgoers and Bill found in his congretation a setting in which he grew comfortably. Pastor Johnson was a mentor whom he trusted.

Pete Johnson told me some time later that he thought Bill had exhibited many of the signs of having a "calling" to the priesthood, but it seemed that it would not be. Bill had done well in college and had met Patty in his first year of law school. Pastor Johnson concluded that Bill's future would center around Patty and the law, not the ministry. However, no matter how busy Bill was, there was always "quality time" for religion.

I had known Patty since her days in the Catholic Youth Organization (CYO). She was always popular, always surrounded by a crowd of friends, always the leader or, better yet, the "spark plug" of her crowd. Patty was fun to be with and gave her all to whatever was happening at the moment, be it confirmation class, a CYO outing, or a bake sale after Mass. Patty had drifted away from weekly Sunday Mass attendance at the beginning of her college career, as her mother told me with a lump in her throat each week. However, she had "come back the stronger," as her mother often misquotes a prediction falsely attributed to me.

"It all started when we were discussing whether to get pre-engaged," Bill continued with his narrative. They both had known how important church was to the other, but it came as a shock to learn that the other prayed seriously and often. They had been sitting in McDonald's. They had just arranged their food, each placing the french fries in the cover of the box their burger came in. Bill had opened the ketchup packet for Patty after watching her struggle with it. Bill finally took a deep breath, wondering how she would react, and asked Patty if it would be okay if they said a little prayer before they ate.

He recalled that she had nodded, and that he had thanked God for their love, for their lives together, and for the McDonald's french fries. "Whenever we pray, now, we always include McDonald's french fries," Patty explained, "It's kind of like a little joke between God and us."

"The joke was on us," Bill continued. It seemed that they each had spent significant time in prayer each day ever since they had been in college. Neither one knew that the other prayed much at all. It was only when they took the risk of praying that afternoon in McDonald's that they were freed up to talk about their own prayer lives. They stayed in McDonald's so long that afternoon, talking about prayer, that they worked up another appetite and each ordered another burger and fries. (Over which they prayed again!)

"That afternoon," Patty explained, "was the best afternoon in both of our lives. We had known that we were very much alike and that we liked the same things, and gradually we had come to know that we loved each other. On that afternoon, however, we came to realize the depth of God's love each of us was experiencing. I knew that I loved Bill, Father, and I knew that God loved Bill. I knew that Bill knew that I loved him, but I didn't know that Bill knew that God loved him . . . does that make sense?"

Bill laughed easily. He recalled how Patty had summed up their lengthy discussion that afternoon in much the same words, ending in the same question. He remembered thinking that everything, the whole world and everything in it, made sense for the very first time. They had each given themselves permission to admit their love for each other and for God. They saw a side, or rather a depth, of each other which was unexpected and, oh, so beautiful.

They read the Bible together regularly after that, and had picked the readings for their wedding even before they knew that they were supposed to. They prayed the lyrics to the music they wanted for their wedding— so much music, in fact, that if it were all to be used the ceremony might have to break for lunch! They recognized the presence of Jesus in everything they saw and did together. They prayed together in each other's church and in each other's arms.

"Father, we belong to different churches, we have a difference in our upbringing and some differences in our faith, but neither of us knows anyone else who experiences Jesus' love exactly the same way we do," Patty said.

Bill continued, "We pray together every day, even if it is just for a couple of minutes." They both marveled at the fact that they had known each other for so long and had kept the most beautiful part of their lives separate. "Sometimes we joke about wondering what else we don't know about each other," one of them said, and the other agreed.

They had not intended to tell me all this, but my offhand remark about Pastor Johnson and myself being able to pray together and my question about whether they could pray together had triggered their self-revelation.

They had opened to me an area very near the core of their being and had trusted me with the beauty of their love. When their story was finished, we all sat back. Someone needed to say what would come next, and I wanted to say it with all my heart, but I held back just long enough to give them the right of invitation.

On behalf of both of them, Bill extended his hands to Patty and to me and asked, quite simply, "Will you pray with us, Father?" There had been tears in my eyes throughout their revelation, but now they were in my throat as well as I held their hands and silently thanked God that there were people like Patty and Bill in the Church. I thanked God that there were people like Pastor Johnson and me as well. When words came, however, I merely thanked God for his presence and his love.

Patty squeezed my hand (and I presumed Bill's) and added quietly, "And thanks especially for McDonald's french fries."

In the doorway on their way out, Bill turned and smiled an almost satirical smile as he winked at Patty and asked her, for my benefit, if now that they had prayed with me, all three of us were "pre-engaged"? I realized then that the definition of pre-engagement had been left up in the air more than an hour earlier. That afternoon, I learned the definition, and so very much more, from Bill and Patty.

They had far to go in working through the difference in their church affiliation as it affected not only their relationship with each other but also their relationship with each other's family of origin and with each other's faith community. Both family and church come with a set of traditions, customs, and practices that provide many particular issues for Bill and Patty to handle. The clearer they were as they worked through these differences, the better off would their children be in years to come.

Yet they were off to a solid start, for they recognized the most basic relationship of all in their lives to be their relationship with God. They knew of God's love for them, not only as individuals but also as a couple striving to reflect his presence and his love in their life together.

I learned the definition of "pre-engagement" that afternoon from Bill and Patty. I had not really learned from them, nor they from each other, of course, for we all had in common the great Teacher who has challenged us, "Learn of me. . . ."

DISCUSSION QUESTIONS:

1. When did you get "pre-engaged"? What happened? Why?

2. What expectations do you have about your interfaith or interdenominational marriage? Where did they come from? Are they real or unreal for you in your relationship now?

3. Have you discussed together your hopes and wishes for passing on your faith to your children? What is your plan?

TWELVE

Substance abuse in the home

Father Robert Tucker

Violence in its many forms has become an increasingly visible and accepted part of our present culture. In many cases alcohol and other substance abuse can be linked to this violence, including suicide and family violence.

No one wants to admit being an alcoholic or an addict or substance abuser. Yet people can pass from wanting a casual drink or joint or "rush" to needing ever increasing amounts, while denying that anything is happening to them. Their personality changes and their behavior becomes increasingly unpredictable, but they do not admit that they have a problem.

It is not only the afflicted person who changes, but also his or her family. Even the person's spouse often enables the problem to continue and even to grow. Those close to the addict sometimes wrongly believe that "if I love him or her more . . ." or "if we get married . . ." or "if I would stop nagging . . ." then the person will change.

It's hard to face the fact that a loved one is an addict or abuser. The sick behavior is allowed to continue and covered up: "Oh, it isn't that bad." "I know in time he or she will change." "Time, responsibility, maturity, children will make a difference."

These are all excuses. Hiding from reality will not bring about a cure or a change in the afflicted person or in the potential harm he or she can and will do. *Perspectives on Marriage*, from ACTA Publications in Chicago, offers some excellent questions for engaged couples to discuss on this problem. I offer a few that are used in many marriage preparation sessions:

1. Do either of you lose time from work because of drinking or using drugs?

2. Is drinking or drug use affecting either of your reputations?

3. Do either of you need to get "high" at a definite time each day or week?

4. Have either of you gotten into financial difficulties as a result of drinking or using drugs?

5. Do either of you drink or take drugs to escape from worries or troubles?

6. Do either of you drink or take drugs to build up your self-confidence?

7. Has alcohol or drugs ever caused either of you to have difficulty sleeping?

8. Have either of you made threats or decisions because of the other's use of alcohol or drugs?

9. Do either of you try to conceal your own or the other's drinking or use of drugs — or deny there is a problem despite strong evidence of its existence?

10. Have either of you ever avoided activities with family and friends because of fear of embarrassment over the other's use of alcohol or drugs?

An affirmative answer to even one of these questions can spell trouble. Another serious issue in marriage is physical abuse. Family violence occurs in every race, religion, age group, and socio-economic class. It is a fact that both sexes suffer from the problem of physical, mental, and verbal abuse. The F.B.I. estimates that there is one wife-beating every four minutes and calls wife-beating the "most unreported crime in the country." Approximately two million abusers take their distress and pain out on their children. Nearly half of the children in the United States have been physically or sexually abused. Five percent of these children have been hospitalized due to the abuse.

All too often we look to the actions of the victim and question, "Why does she stay?" or "Why does he let her do this?" We must move from these questions about the victim and see how our culture and society, with their stress on power, control and security, keep the victim trapped and immobilized.

Some suggestions about physical and substance abuse in marriage:

1. Realize you cannot change the habits of another.
Be honest. You know how difficult it is to change your own bad habits. You can challenge your spouse to growth and personal discipline and maturity, but he or she must accept the challenge — before the engagement and not after the wedding! If this problem exists in your relationship, *delay the wedding and address the problem first!*

2. Be aware of attitudes and biases within yourself that may interfere with your own growth and awareness of these situations and problems.
You can only hope to change the attitudes and behaviors of others by first changing those within yourself.

3. Seek professional help.
If a problem exists with drugs, alcohol or physical abuse, then don't hide it. Otherwise you will become an "enabler" or a "co-dependent."

Before a couple gets married is the right time to share with a future spouse any alcohol/drug abuse or physical/sexual abuse which may have occurred in one's own family of origin. It means taking a risk and trusting the other person not to be judgmental. Talking about such problems with someone we love is important, and bringing it out in the open can start us on a path to healing. Such history can also serve as a point of reference for a couple so they can be aware of any negative patterns they may adopt from their own families.

Marrying out of fear or dependence can never truly be a marriage. Take the time to really get to know yourself. And share that knowledge with your future spouse, along with any concerns you may have. Now is the time to do it. It can be a wonderful opportunity for healing and growth.

DISCUSSION QUESTIONS:

1. Do you bring any learned behaviors about alcohol, addictions, or abuse to your new life together? Are these behaviors good for your relationship? Explain.

2. Do you want to change any patterns or behaviors either of you may have in these areas? What do you need to do to accomplish that?

3. What are you most afraid of in your relationship?

THIRTEEN

Balancing marriage and career

Father Robert Tucker

Most of us wear many hats, carry many responsibilities, face many challenges, and have many decisions to make. This means we have to select the areas to which we devote our time, concern, and expertise. It is difficult to give a one hundred percent performance in all the areas of our daily life.

Too often our personal sense of self-worth is based on what we do rather than on who we are. In a society so concerned with how many degrees we have, where we work, and what successes we can boast of, we can forget that we are people with needs and desires and that we must sometimes face choices between doing the task and being a person.

In our contemporary society we run the risk of being controlled by our likes, dislikes, wants, fears, doubts, and dreams, and of letting our will power and our spiritual and intellectual lives take a back seat. If we think we can do little, we are in danger of doing nothing.

Some places of employment and certain types of careers expect more than seventy hours of work a week. How can we fit a spouse and children into this kind of lifestyle? When is it a good time to have a child? When is it a good time to make a decision that our marriage will come before our careers? How high on the corporate ladder do we need or desire to climb?

These are questions married couples need to discuss. In the Gospels, Jesus asks us to share all we have and challenges us to question ourselves when we think we need everything right NOW.

But this doesn't come naturally. We want more. We work beyond our human endurance level to stockpile for the house, car, or trip. Yet we are also blessed persons. We would like to share our giftedness and unique personhood with another in a good marriage. We want to share our love with a child or two, or maybe even three or four — but how do we do it all?

Here are some suggestions for all couples who want to meet the challenge of balancing marriage and career:

1. **Talk with yourself and your conscience.**
   Know yourself and your desires and pray over them. Reflect on the "Our Father." It can help us be open to the Lord's will.

2. **Talk with your spouse of daily joys, problems, and frustrations. Share in a creative, loving way with each other.**
   What is best for the two of you? How can you be real to yourselves and not only to your careers or your employers?

3. **Be aware of the increasing need for strength of character.**
   It takes faith and will power to say no to the pressures and demands of the world and to put your marriage, relationship, and family first. It may require the rediscovery of basic values that have been obscured by the supposed "good life." It may mean you will not conform to the crowd in the size of your home, the brand of your car, the clubs you join, and trips that you take.

4. **Don't equate "have" with how you feel about yourselves.**
   Does the need for the latest gadgets or the attitude of keeping up with the Joneses really help you to feel better about yourselves as individuals? What is your own personal worth as a person? Is it based on what you do or who you are?

5. **Decide what is indispensable in your life.**
   Do you take the time to "buy" the best of love, joy, and values for each other? This is not purchased in a store but in time together, and it is top of the line.

6. **Keep yourselves from getting bored.**

   Will you expend real effort to stimulate your relationship? Without special time together, sensitivity to real values and love can be lost and the manners and social graces behind compassion will be nowhere to be found. Do you wish to live as roommates or coworkers or as lovers in love?

7. **Don't have an exclusive orientation to the present.**

   Today is not all, or even the best, you have to offer. Don't let long-term goals for a better tomorrow get lost in the business of today.

8. **Live your faith, don't just record it in a book.**

   Faith needs to be manifested in a person's choices and being. It requires time, daily prayer, participation in Sunday Eucharist, and assisting in one's parish family. Does eternal life and the Gospel message give you any drive or mission purpose for your marriage? Perhaps you feel that you may be able to do only a little. But that "little" may be the key to your eternal life.

DISCUSSION QUESTIONS

1. Given the choices you are making regarding how you spend your time, energy, and money, what are the values you are exhibiting at this point in your life together? Would you like to see a change?

2. What little thing could you do right now to help bring your choices in line with what you claim to value?

3. How are you going to keep the balance in your life after you are married?

FOURTEEN

Money management

Sandra Maineri

When lives and values merge with marriage and young couples make plans for every single aspect of their new lifestyle, money management should certainly not be overlooked.

Mitch is a construction worker enrolled part-time in the evening division of a local university, working toward a degree in business. He was raised, as he admits, "in the prehistoric days when you never talked about money or never knew your parents' income and obligations." He remembers manila envelopes with cash assigned to pay certain bills. Transactions were rarely noted. Unexpected emergencies created financial chaos, and his parents were "frugal and pessimistic" about money.

Diana, Mitch's wife, is an L.P.N. working full-time in a hospital. Her father was a career military man. Her family never had a lot of money, but they had an "open, diplomatic way of setting financial goals."

Once when Diana and her sister desperately wanted a pony, the family reviewed its priorities and expenses, added to its income through a part-time job for the mother, and actually bought a pony!

Mitch and Diana don't always see eye to eye on expenses. Diana feels that if you want something and have the income, you should get it. She has expressed this feeling about home ownership, furnishings, and vacations. She sees nothing wrong with using credit from time to time.

Even though Mitch earns a more than adequate income, he still has a "doomsday" approach to debt. He'd like to remain debt-free, put off vacations, save, and "make do."

More than money is involved when couples sit down to talk about financial issues in their marriage. But there are some monetary rules of thumb that anyone could apply to these decisions.

The first is to know the difference between "needs" and "wants." Everyone requires transportation, for example, but there are new and used cars, sports and imports, motorcycles and mopeds, public transportation and van pooling. If the object is to get from one place to another on a regular basis, all options should be considered. A second car in a family may cost $5,000 per year or more to operate, based upon car payments, insurance, taxes, registration, gas, and maintenance. This money, once spent on transportation, is no longer available for other areas of the budget. That is why it is important to really define "needs."

For example, how much new clothing is necessary? Must all furnishings be new? How about entertainment? Does the couple have a plan for savings and insurance? In other words, are all bases covered with the current income?

BUDGET. The word strikes as much terror into the hearts of couples as the word "diet" to an out-of-control eater. But really, a budget is nothing more than a plan for the use of one's money. In a budget, couples set mutual goals, both long and short term. They figure out their disposable take-home pay and their monthly expenses. They make a plan for their discretionary (what's left over) income. They know where their money goes. "If you have $85 in your wallet on Monday and $40 on Friday, you should remember how you spent the $45," insists Mitch.

Now, about the unpredictable. Of course unplanned things happen. Mitch and Diana learned the town planned to put sewers in their neighborhood. It would cost property owners thousands of dollars each. Yipes, an emergency! But Diana and Mitch had agreed not to spend every penny of their income. They knew it was wise to establish an emergency fund — a type of savings account used only for unforeseen events and equal to three months of their combined take-home pay.

Although this would not cover the cost of the sewers, the couple had enough for the hook-up and lots to spare. The town billed them ten percent of the remaining cost per year for ten years, but their budget could readily incorporate the new expense because they had been wise enough to leave a large part of their income as discretionary. They merely redirected these funds for a while. They cut down a bit on luxuries and entertaining, shaved their food expenses by eating out less frequently, and made a concerted effort to buy clothes only when needed and on sale.

Mitch and Diana's finances may change radically in the next few years. He hopes to finish college and establish his own business. The couple plans to have children. They will probably acquire a few more pieces of furniture and finish paying off one of their cars. Other unexpected expenses will undoubtedly arise, but their income will also improve, and they will have settled in with each other and be more used to each other's money management habits.

Luckily they have an income that covers their fixed expenses such as housing, car payments, insurance, and heat. They have figured out how to reduce food, clothing, and entertainment expenses. They have added a savings plan for vacations, and their emergency fund is used only for the unexpected.

Mitch no longer fears overwhelming debt in their future, and Diana is now proud of their budgeting. When values and lives merge with marriage, attitudes about finances eventually do too.

DISCUSSION QUESTIONS:

1. What has your family of origin taught you about money management? Were there any rules (spoken or unspoken) in your family about money? Can you name them?

2. What happens when you and your future spouse sit down to talk about money? Are you bringing any non-negotiables to the table?

3. What do you need to do to enable yourself and your future spouse to create your own money management style?

OTHER RESOURCES FOR ENGAGED COUPLES

Beginning Your Marriage, 7th Edition by John L. Thomas. This classic and comprehensive book has been used by more than 3,500,000 couples to help them prepare for their marriage.

176 pp., paper, $3.50

Perspectives on Marriage. A workbook of gentle exercises, discussion material, and practical information designed to to facilitate communication between couples on the key issues of their individual marriage.

Ecumenical Edition: 72 pp., 8 1/2 x 11" paper, $3.25

Catholic Edition: 80 pp., 8 1/2 x 11" paper, $3.50

What Kind of Marriage. Here is a new dramatic video story on the issues involved in marriage for use by engaged couples as well as those considering marriage as a remote possibility. Comes with Discussion Guide.

30-minute video tape with Discussion Guide, $39.95

Available from Christian booksellers or call 1-800-397-2282.